FOLK FINISHES

This desk with matching chair (also illustrated on the front cover) has been decorated with a brown ocher vinegar glaze over a bright yellow background and details in blue-green acrylic paint. (Collection of Tom Kennedy)

FOLK FINISHES

WHAT THEY ARE AND HOW TO CREATE THEM

RUBENS TELES
JAMES ADAMS

VIKING STUDIO BOOKS

We dedicate this book to the painters of early
America, who have left such a wonderful
legacy of decorative techniques and painted
objects; to our families for their perpetual
love and support of our creative energies; and
especially to the memory of Jay Johnson and
Robert Bishop, who inspired us and led us to
this work, which we are now pleased to be
able to share with others.

VIKING STUDIO BOOKS

Published by the Penguin Group
Penguin Books USA Inc., 375 Hudson Street,
New York, New York, 10014, U.S.A.

Penguin Books Ltd, 27 Wrights Lane,
London W8 5TZ, England

Penguin Books Australia Ltd, Ringwood,
Victoria, Australia

Penguin Books Canada Ltd, 2801 John Street,
Markham, Ontario, Canada L3R 1B4

Penguin Books (N.Z.) Ltd, 182-90 Wairau Road,
Auckland 10, New Zealand

Penguin Books Ltd, Registered Offices:
Harmondsworth, Middlesex, England

First published by Viking Studio Books, an imprint of Penguin Books USA Inc.

First printing, October 1994
10 9 8 7 6 5 4 3 2 1

Copyright © Rubens Teles and James Adams 1994
All rights reserved

Library of Congress
Catalog Card Number: 93-85351

Book designed by Nancy Danahy
Printed and bound by Dai Nippon Printing Co., Hong Kong, Ltd.

ISBN: 0-525-48588-0

C O N T E N T S

ACKNOWLEDGMENTS

A very special acknowledgment must be given to the late Henry Niemann in recognition of his enthusiastic help in the early stages of this project, which was of such interest to him. We regret that it is not possible for him to see the book completed.

Thanks are also due to the many persons whose interest in our work has been so encouraging. They are: Alexander and Annabelle Barrett; Milton Bond; Cullman & Kravis, Inc.; Toni and Aymon DeMauro; Burton and Helaine Fendelman; David Guilmet for Bell/Guilmet Design; Anne G. Harris; Stephanie and Robert Tardell; Tom Kennedy; Victor Niederhoffer; Olde Hope Antiques, New Hope, Pennsylvania; Grace and Bill Ryan; and several private collectors.

Gregory Tavarone deserves our thanks for the many series of step-by-step photographs that illustrate this book; and our editor, Cyril I. Nelson, has been unstinting in his help in making sure that the book would prove a credit to us.

INTRODUCTION

Throughout the eighteenth century and past the middle of the nineteenth, the practice of imitative painting techniques, including graining, marbleizing, and fantasy finishes, was widespread—initially, among the colonists, and later, among the citizens of the young nation. Inasmuch as the fine woods and marble used by city cabinetmakers were too expensive for the majority, the methods of faux painting that are discussed and illustrated in this book offered an economical means of visually transforming such modest materials as pine and maple to simulate the mahogany, rosewood, and marble that were used in high-style furniture.

Because there were no schools in early America where one might learn the techniques of graining and marbleizing, and because there were few apprenticeships with the cabinetmakers of the time, each craftsman had to rely on his own resourcefulness and imagination to discover the paints, tools, and techniques necessary to create the visual transforma- resulted in broad and wonder- tations of wood grains and the and paints were often home- were as varied as the minds tions. These craft experiments ful variations on and represen- splendor of marble. Brushes made, and the painted finishes and hands of their creators.

In the late twentieth cen- growing interest in decorative access to abundant informa- the creation of faux finishes. in finding economical ways to And what should be of chief book is not to pursue a slavish trated, but rather—once hav- techniques and tools described fact that imagination, experi- the freedom of creativity are values to be found in any tury, with the renewed and painted surfaces, we have tion about and approaches to Once again we are interested achieve stylish visual effects. interest to those who use this imitation of the effects illus- ing learned and used the basic here—to realize and value the mentation, spontaneity, and probably the most important artistic pursuit. Have faith in

The body of this miniature chest of drawers is decorated with a burnt sienna vinegar glaze over a yellow background, and the marbleized top has dark green and black vinegar glazes over a white undercoat. (Private collection)

yourself and in your own inherent aesthetic abilities, and the information contained in this volume will help clarify your creative vision.

The late Dr. Robert Bishop, the longtime Director of the Museum of American Folk Art in New York City, was a man who inspired and empowered so many during his career. He was noted for saying: "Don't ever say you can't do something. Just try what you hope for and you will do it."

RUBENS TELES
JAMES ADAMS

CHAPTER 1:
BEFORE WE BEGIN TO PAINT—
THESE ARE THE BASICS TO BE LEARNED

It is important to select a workspace spacious enough to accommodate the spattering of thin liquid glazes. A cool, ventilated place is best, for you will be using polyurethane. If you use powder pigments, it is also important to use a mask and thin latex gloves, for some colors should not be inhaled or touched. Be sure to use a large drop cloth on the floor.

Avoid working in humid weather, for if you do, the glaze may either bubble or bead up and disappear within a few minutes after application. Brushing the glaze back and forth until the surface is totally covered will overcome this problem. You may then proceed with your design. On humid days, you must allow additional time (about ten minutes) for the glaze and varnish to dry. To remove an unsatisfactory design before varnishing the piece, moisten a paper towel with vinegar, wipe the piece clean, and then repeat the procedure. A piece cannot be reworked after it has been varnished unless you cover the varnish with BIN or some other alcohol-base (*not water-base*) primer.

TOOLS

These are the tools you will need in order to create any of the design patterns in this book.

1. Badger

A soft natural-bristle brush either 3" or 4" wide that is used to spread the glaze. Currently, a Badger costs about $120.00. A Badger is very efficient in spreading glaze and preventing beading. As an economical alternative, any other natural-bristle brush will do.

2. Brushes

Two or three 2"-wide nylon-bristle brushes to be used for water-base (acrylic) paints.

3. Four- or five-headed brush (a.k.a. pencil grainer)

This is used for fine-detail work on grained pieces, such as making knots on wood and creating striped effects. Multiheaded brushes can also be made by cutting away sections of the bristles on any 3" or 4"-wide brush to form "teeth." The remaining bristles should be pulled together with Scotch tape, thus creating the multiple heads.

4. 1" artist brush

This is used with water-base paint for painting scenes and coloring the finer details on pieces.

5. #0/2, #0, #3, #5, and #7 artist brushes

These are used with water-base paint to create a variety of details when painting scenes or fine lines on decorated pieces.

6. Feather

A natural bird's feather, such as that of a duck or chicken. They may be purchased in most art-supply stores. Pointed feathers are the best.

7. Natural sponge

Natural sponges can be purchased in hardware, art supply, and bath stores.

Natural sponges are better to use than ordinary artificial kitchen sponges, which are too flat to create the patterned effects desired.

8. Combs

Metal or hard-leather combs or corrugated cardboard are equally useful.

9. Brush for polyurethane finish

Polyurethane brushes should be approximately 2" to 4" wide, depending on the size and shape of the object.

10. Candle

This is used for smoke graining. A no-drip candle is recommended for this type of graining.

11. Sandblock

To be used for antiquing effects.

12. Linseed-oil putty

Linseed-oil putty is used for creating designs over the glaze because the putty does not mix with the glaze. Therefore, when the linseed-oil putty touches the glaze, the result looks like seaweed.

13. BIN or other alcohol-base primer

BIN is an alcohol-base primer that is applied on the piece to be decorated before the base coat, and it allows you to paint on metal, plastic, and other nonporous surfaces, as well as on surfaces that have been previously painted (whether with oil- or water-base paints).

14. How to clean and care for your brushes

Brushes should be thoroughly washed with soap and water until entirely free of paint, then dried by shaking them outside the working area. To store them properly, stand the brushes on their handles and keep the bristles straight.

Brushes used to apply polyurethane must be cleaned with mineral spirits or turpentine. You may prefer to use inexpensive brushes that can simply be thrown away after use.

A well-made varnish brush provides a very fine, slick finish. Prices vary from a few dollars to many hundreds depending on one's purpose. Expensive brushes are not necessary, however. The personnel at local paint stores can help in making selections. For a slick finish, sand lightly between each coat of polyurethane after it has dried thoroughly.

The brush used to apply the BIN primer should be cleaned *only with ammonia*. Since BIN is an alcohol-base paint, do not use mineral spirits, turpentine, or water to clean the brush. Priming a few pieces at a time with a disposable brush may prove the most effective and economical way of priming.

THE GLAZE

The glaze is composed of three ingredients.

1. Karo syrup, light or dark

If Karo syrup is unavailable in local supermarkets or grocery stores, molasses or honey are good substitutes. This ingredient binds the glaze. Use sparingly. Karo syrup will never dry if used in large quantities. A 1/4 teaspoon of syrup is all that is necessary to bind the powder pigment and the vinegar together. It is important not to exceed the recommended amount of Karo syrup. To achieve a denser glaze, use more pigment; for a more liquid glaze, use more vinegar. *The amount of Karo always remains the same.* If you use too much Karo, the glaze will be shiny after it dries. Using the proper amount of Karo syrup (1/4 teaspoon) will result in a glaze that appears flat after drying.

2. Vinegar

Vinegar is used instead of water to create a glaze because it is more reactive to the materials.

3. Powder pigment

Although there are many varieties of dry pigment, Grumbacher is perhaps the most satisfactory. Powder pigments seem to be easier to work with, but you can also use dry poster paint, or a concentrated paste paint available at Guerra Paint that works just as well. More paste paint is usually needed because the paste paint is weaker than the powder pigments. Colors always have identical names regardless of the brand name used (ocher, raw sienna, burnt umber, etc.).

PRACTICING

Although many people prefer to practice the various painting techniques on pieces of wood before painting a piece of furniture, it is not really necessary, for individual pieces of furniture often dictate specific creative impressions to the artist by virtue of their form and size. Experience reveals that the inspiration for creating design patterns generally changes with each piece. Color schemes and design patterns are often the result of the worker's momentary mood. A relaxed attitude usually yields the best results.

THE POLYURETHANE FINISH

Protecting a finished piece is important. Since the glaze has a vinegar base, it never really dries, even though it seems to. Water or vinegar will ruin your decorated finish if the glaze has not been sealed properly. Protect finished pieces by applying two or three thin coats of polyurethane. Polyurethane dries faster when it has been applied in thin coats.

Since polyurethane is difficult to remove, *seal your piece only when you are completely satisfied with it.* Any change can be made before you apply the polyurethane finish, *for the glaze can easily be removed by wiping it with a rag soaked in vinegar,* even weeks after the glaze has been applied. Returning to the original base color makes it possible for you to rework a new design from the beginning.

It is important to note that a water-base polyurethane cannot be used as the sealer; *only an oil-base polyurethane should be used.*

However, even after you have sealed the piece with polyurethane, it can be repainted if the results prove unsatisfactory. Begin the process again by painting the object with BIN. This is an alcohol-base primer that adheres to any surface and successfully covers everything you have done, thus allowing you to start all over again. Then go to your base color and proceed as before. For a smooth finish, remove the undesired glaze and varnish with any paint stripper (acrylic or oil) and restart your project.

WHERE TO OBTAIN MATERIALS

In New York City, Pearl Paint, 308 Canal Street, New York, NY 10013; 212-431-7932 or (800-221-6845), has all the material necessary to reproduce any design pattern illustrated in this book. A mail-order catalog may be obtained over the telephone from outside New York City. Also based in New York City is Guerra Paint and Pigment, 510 East 13th Street at Avenue A, New York, NY 10009; 212-529-0628 or 718-388-5213. Both establishments have a full line of paints and pigments in powder

and paste form that can be purchased through mail order. Janovic Plaza, also in New York City, Third Avenue at 67th Street, 10021; 212-772-1400, has a full line of top-quality acrylic paint, polyurethane, brushes, and an excellent selection of graining tools.

MATERIALS NEEDED

1. Putty

DAP painter's putty (linseed-oil putty)

2. Cloths

tackcloth, rags, newspapers, paper towels

3. Paint

water-base wall paint in semigloss colors (red, green, yellow, blue, black, and "off white"). Ask your paint store for the best brand of paint.

4. Powder pigment

Colors: Burnt umber (gray-brown), Indian red (barn red), yellow ocher (mustard yellow), chromium opaque (old green), Van Dyke brown (brown-brown), ivory black (jet black), or any other color of your choice.

5. Vinegar

regular white kitchen vinegar

6. Syrup

Karo syrup (white or dark)

7. Primer

regular primer for unpainted wood, or BIN (an alcohol-base primer) if you are painting over metal, formica, or any other nonporous surfaces.

8. Polyurethane finish

Last 'N Last, Minwax, or Basic Quick 15. If none of these can be found, choose another oil-base polyurethane. IMPORTANT: *Do not use a water-base polyurethane.*

9. Shoe polish

large cans of brown and black

10. Steel wool

various thicknesses

11. Cans/Jars

small to medium sizes in which to mix glazes

CHAPTER II: GRAINING

INGREDIENTS

BIN, or other alcohol-base or acrylic primer

Acrylic semigloss paint (yellow or red)

Karo syrup (light or dark)

powder pigment

white vinegar

oil-base polyurethane (Last 'N Last, Minwax, or Basic Quick 15)

TOOLS

3 or more inexpensive 2" to 3"-wide natural-bristle brushes (one for the
primer, one for the polyurethane, and one for the application of each glaze
color to be used)

1 2" to 3"-wide nylon-bristle brush (for acrylic paint)

1 Badger—this and other background brushes are used to create patterns

1 multiheaded brush (a.k.a. pencil grainer)

1 metal graining comb

1 piece of stiff corrugated cardboard

1 overgrainer (a stiff nylon-bristle brush that creates grainlike striations when
dragged over the wet glaze

1 *natural* sponge

1 small can of painter's putty (DAP or other linseed-oil putty)

1 pair of thin latex gloves (**important**)

PRIMING

Before painting, prime the piece of furniture with BIN or any other alcohol-base or acrylic primer. Do *not* sand the piece if an antique look is desired. Unsanded wood will show imperfections in the final product. Sandpapering produces a smooth, slick effect.

UNDERPAINTING

Paint the object with acrylic semigloss red or yellow paint (fig. 1), depending on the type of wood that you wish to simulate (i.e. yellow for maple, oak, and cherry; red for mahogany, rosewood, and ebony). Choose a bright tone of either color, as the glaze you are going to apply over it will darken the base coat. Let it dry well. Acrylic paint usually dries in about twenty to thirty minutes. For a fine finish, coat the object twice with the semigloss paint, sanding lightly between each application. Applying a semigloss finish is important. The glaze will then slide on the smooth surface, making it easy to work.

GLAZE PREPARATION   Prepare the glaze mixture out of the three basic components: corn syrup (light or dark Karo syrup is recommended), white vinegar, and powder pigments. The glaze should be of a color that contrasts with the base coat, and which, when applied over the base coat, approximates the colors of the wood that you plan to imitate. A clear glass or plastic jar enables easy observation of the mixing process, but any small container will do. Begin with 1/4 teaspoon of Karo syrup, to which you will add 1 teaspoon or more of the powder pigment. A small brush works best as it mixes the ingredients to a thick paste quickly. When thoroughly mixed, add approximately 2 tablespoons of white vinegar. Colors may be lightened or darkened by adding white, gray, or black pigment. To revive a dry glaze, add vinegar. The glaze can be thickened by adding more pigment or liquified by adding more vinegar. When using light-color pigments, you may need a larger quantity of pigment, and when using dark-color pigments, a smaller quantity.

GRAINING   Begin the graining technique by applying the glaze to a small area with a 2" to 3"-wide natural-bristle brush or a Badger, brushing on the glaze until it is very smooth and semitransparent. The glaze takes about five minutes to dry under normal circumstances, so you will have time to decide on the desired design motif, in case you have not already done so. It is important to apply the glaze to an area small enough to be worked comfortably within the fast drying time of the glaze (fig. 2). For example, on a chest of drawers, do the top, then one side, then the other side, and then each drawer in succession. When you work in this manner, the glaze will not dry out too quickly, and you won't be doing more brushing than necessary. If the glaze should dry too soon, go over the glaze with a brush that is slightly wet with vinegar, and it will be ready to work again.

1 *Paint a surface with an acrylic base color and allow it to dry.*

2 *Apply a vinegar glaze with a Badger. Because the glaze must remain wet during this part of the process, work only a small portion of the surface at a time.*

Once the surface is covered with glaze, drag a brush, a scrunched-up towel, a torn piece of corrugated cardboard, or an overgrainer over it to create diagonal lines (fig. 3). This will result in the removal of some of the glaze and create a striped effect. Twitch your hand slightly while dragging the implement to give a more convincing grained effect (fig. 4). To obtain a light-and-dark striped effect, go over some area of the graining with a paper towel with some vinegar on it, to remove more glaze here and there. On one of the light areas, using a five-headed brush, dab on dense pigment. Tilt the jar to expose the pigment under the vinegar (figs. 5a, 5b). This very dense glaze will be almost like paint. Create the knots and grain with the five-headed brush (figs. 6–8) and add knots at various intervals for a balanced effect (figs. 9–11). Extensive detail work results in a more realistic finish. Less detail work results in a more folky look.

BURL WOOD

Repeat the above process, but in some areas, with a vertically held brush, twist the brush over the wet glaze to create the illusion of round knots or burl wood. If the glaze is dry, use a brush with a *little* vinegar. As a final touch of realism, collect the settled pigment, and using a four-headed brush, trace lines around each knot.

POLYURETHANE FINISH

Do **NOT** apply the polyurethane finish if you desire to erase your work, should you be dissatisfied with it. To remove the unsatisfactory glaze pattern use a paper towel or rag saturated with vinegar. The semigloss base coat will eventually reappear. If, however, you are satisfied with the finished design, then apply the polyurethane. Apply with an inexpensive natural-bristle brush. Two or three light coats are sufficient. Allow the first coat to dry thoroughly—about two hours on a dry day—before applying the second coat. Follow the instructions on the can.

Because you have been using a water-soluble glaze, contact with anything wet will remove the glazed design until the polyurethane finish has been applied. Polyurethane provides good water-repellant protection and will render a glossy or satin finish, depending on the type used. If you prefer to give your piece an antique look, consult Chapter VII for the process to be followed.

3 *Simultaneously drag and shake an overgrainer through the wet-glazed surface to create a portion of the grain pattern.*

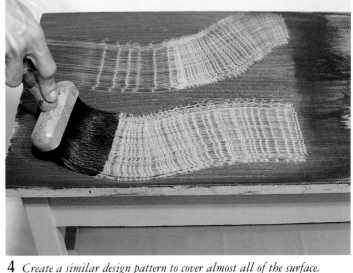

4 *Create a similar design pattern to cover almost all of the surface.*

5a *Tilt the glass container to expose the powder pigment at the bottom.*

5b *Pick up some of the pigment with a brush having five teeth.*

6 *Paint knot designs in the areas between the grained lines.*

7 *Paint knot designs in the areas between the grained lines.*

8 *Paint circles or ovals around the knot designs.*

7

9 *Add knots at various intervals for a balanced effect.*

10 *Add knots at various intervals for a balanced effect.*

11 *Add knots at various intervals for a balanced effect.*

12 *Here is the finished table illustrating the grained design.*

An Empire pedestal table of c. 1825 with a contemporary finish. Burnt sienna has been applied over an ocher base coat to create the appearance of bird's-eye maple.

Side table with graining in burnt sienna over a yellow background. Green and yellow freehand designs complete the decoration—see the details.

Detail of side table showing graining on the drawer and freehand swag decoration.

Detail of side table showing free-hand tassel decoration on the front and side.

Detail showing a drawer grained with a glaze of burnt sienna over a yellow background.

Pennsylvania kas of the early 19th century. The doors are sponged and grained in Venetian red over a yellow base. The trim around the doors is a blue glaze sponged over an off-white. The artist is David Guilmet for Bell/Guilmet Design. (Photograph courtesy Olde Hope Antiques, New Hope, Pennsylvania)

This contemporary built-in bar unit by David Guilmet for Bell/Guilmet Design is painted burnt orange with doors grained in raw umber over an ocher background. (Photograph courtesy Olde Hope Antiques, New Hope, Pennsylvania)

This drop-leaf table, which is decorated on top with an oval scene painting, has a raw umber vinegar glaze over maroon underpainting and borders in blue-green and yellow.

C H A P T E R   I I I :   M A R B L E I Z I N G

INGREDIENTS

BIN, or other alcohol-base or acrylic primer

Acrylic semigloss paint (white or off-white)

Karo syrup (light or dark)

powder pigment

white vinegar

oil-base polyurethane (Last 'N Last, Minwax, or Basic Quick 15)

TOOLS

3 or more inexpensive 2" to 3"-wide natural-bristle brushes (one for the primer, one for the polyurethane, and one for the application of each glaze color to be used)

1 2" to 3"-wide nylon-bristle brush (for acrylic paint)

1 Badger—this and other background brushes are used to create patterns

2 artist brushes—a thick one (#3) for creating wide veins and a thinner one (#0) for secondary veins. Bristles should be fairly stiff for best results.

1 *natural* sponge

1 natural feather (a pointed feather is the best)

1 pair of thin latex gloves (**important**)

PRIMING

Before painting, prime the piece of furniture with BIN or any other alcohol-base or acrylic primer. Do *not* sand the piece if an antique look is desired. Unsanded wood will show imperfections in the final product. Sandpapering produces a smooth, slick effect.

UNDERPAINTING

Paint the object with acrylic semigloss white or off-white paint (fig. 1). For a fine finish, coat the object twice with the semigloss paint, sanding lightly between each application. Applying a semigloss finish is important. The glaze will not only slide on the semigloss paint making it easy to work, but the smooth surface will also help to achieve a remarkable facsimile of marble.

GLAZE PREPARATION AND APPLICATION

Prepare two separate glaze mixtures, one red and one gray. The glaze is made out of three components: corn syrup (light or dark Karo syrup is recommended), white vinegar, and powder pigments. A clear glass or plastic jar enables easy observation of the mixing process, but any small container will do. Begin with 1/4 teaspoon of Karo syrup, to which you will add 1 teaspoon or more of powder pigment. A small brush works best as it mixes the ingredients to a thick paste quickly. When thoroughly mixed, add approximately 2 tablespoons of white vinegar. Colors may be lightened or darkened by adding white, gray, or black pigment. To revive a dry glaze add vinegar. The glaze can be thickened by adding more pigment or liquified by adding more vinegar. When using light-color pigments, you may need a larger quantity of pigment, and when using dark-color pigments, a smaller quantity.

Apply the red and gray glazes to the surface in an irregular, diagonal stripe pattern, with a 2" to 3"-wide natural-bristle brush or a Badger (fig. 2). If the glaze bubbles or beads up and does not stick to the surface, continue brushing back and forth in long strokes. Tilting the container, which holds the glaze, sideways produces more pigment thus revealing a thicker consistency of glaze. After the glazes have been applied (fig. 3), lightly dab the entire surface with a damp sponge, blending the two colors (fig. 4). The result should be a blended but subtly striped and mottled design (fig. 5).

VEINING

Major veins should be applied in roughly the same direction as the first striping. Drag a small #3 artist brush saturated with vinegar over the surface (fig. 6). Then blot the surface with a dry paper towel (fig. 7). Applying heavy pressure while dragging the brush will result in prominent veins. Weaker veins are produced with less pressure. Vinegar lifts the glaze, so by wetting your brush in vinegar, you are able to continue making as many veins as desired (fig. 8). For best results, avoid making the veins too symmetrical. Asymmetrical lines help avoid a painted look. Then add smaller veins for balance. Smaller secondary veins feed into the primary veins that are always painted first. With your smallest #0 artist brush dipped in vinegar, make secondary veins that are roughly parallel to the larger ones (fig. 9). Veins should meet at oblique angles. Avoid crisscrossing veins, for a crisscross pattern is not usually found in marble. The more vinegar that is used, the stronger the impression of the vein becomes. To add greater realism, press down on the brush in a twisting motion so that the vein has an irregular pattern. When painting the top of a piece of furniture, it is important to continue the veining over the edges, matching the color and contour of each vein (figs. 10, 11).

SPOTTING

Some types of marble have white spots. Apply drops of vinegar throughout to achieve a spotted effect (fig. 12). Dab with a dry paper towel (fig. 13). If an additional color is desired, mix a glaze and with a feather that has been dipped in the glaze, paint veins over the previous ones. This technique will produce a very complex and interesting pattern.

1 *Paint the surface to be marbleized with white or off-white acrylic paint. Let it dry thoroughly.*

2 *Brush the vinegar glaze over the base coat in alternating stripes of color.*

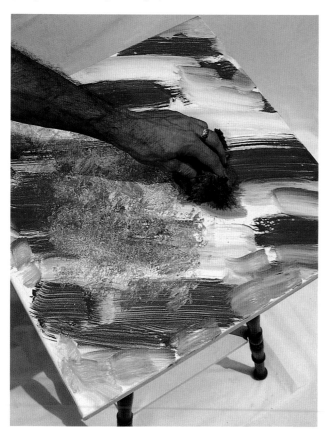

3 *Dab a natural sponge over the wet glaze.*

4 *Continue dabbing until the stripes are almost completely blended as illustrated in figure 5.*

5 *The table top after the sponge blending has been completed.*

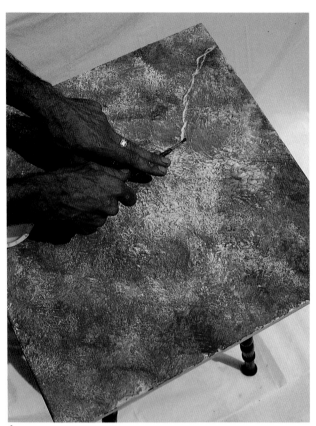

6 *Wet a #3 brush with vinegar. Roll the brush while dragging it over the surface to create a line of veining.*

7 *Dab the wet line with a small piece of paper towel to lift some glaze and thus define the vein.*

8 *Add more veins as desired, maintaining a similar direction between them.*

9 *The table top showing the sponge blending and veins.*

10 *Continue the veins over the edges of the table for a more realistic look.*

11 *Paint veins on all sides of the table top.*

12 *Dab drops of vinegar over the glaze to create white spots.*

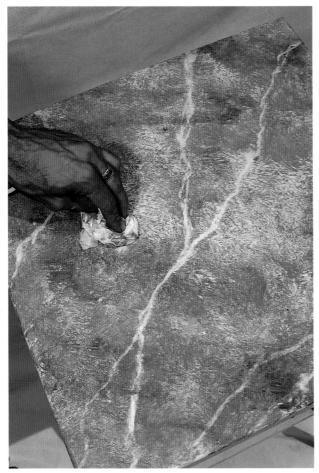

13 *Blot the vinegar drops with a dry paper towel to add definition.*

14 *Here is the finished marbleized table top and shelf.*

POLYURETHANE FINISH

Do **NOT** apply the polyurethane finish if you desire to erase your work, should you be dissatisfied with it. To remove the unsatisfactory glaze pattern use a paper towel or a rag saturated with vinegar. The semigloss white base coat will eventually reappear. If, however, you are satisfied with the finished design, then apply the polyurethane. Apply with an inexpensive natural-bristle brush. Two or three light coats are sufficient. Allow the first coat to dry thoroughly—about two hours on a dry day—before applying the second coat. Follow the instructions on the can.

Because you have been using a water-soluble glaze, contact with anything wet will remove the glazed design until the polyurethane finish has been applied. Inasmuch as the marbleizing technique simulates a polished surface, the clear, glossy look given by the polyurethane creates a perfect finish. If you prefer to give your piece an antique look, consult Chapter VII for the process to be followed.

An octagon box that has been marbleized with an ocher vinegar glaze over a yellow background.

This detail of the octagon box shows the green and black veining made with a thin wet brush.

The top of this coffee table is marbleized with orange and yellow vinegar glazes over an off-white undercoat, and the legs have been antiqued in an off-white acrylic with gold details.

The bowl of this ceramic lamp is marbleized with chromium oxide green and black glazes and a mahogany glaze above and below. Additional detailing has been done in black and gold acrylics. (Made for Cullman & Kravis, Inc.)

The top of this drop-leaf table has green and black glazes over an off-white base coat. The legs are painted black.

Detail of the top of the drop-leaf table.

This whatnot shelf is marbleized with chromium oxide green and gray vinegar glazes over a white undercoat.

The top of this candlestand is marbleized with a veridian green vinegar glaze over a white background, and the legs are mahoganized with a black vinegar glaze over rust-red paint.

Two views of bathroom walls that have been marbleized with chromium opaque green and gray glazes over a white background. (Residence of Stephanie and Robert Tardell)

Two views of an entrance hall where the moldings are marbleized with veridian green and black vinegar glazes over a white background. The detail of the door shows a door frame in faux walnut graining (raw umber vinegar glaze over a yellow background) and door panels marbleized with veridian green and ocher glazes over a white background.

CHAPTER IV: FANTASY FINISHES

INGREDIENTS

BIN, or other alcohol-base or acrylic primer

Acrylic semigloss paint (colors of your choice)

Karo syrup (light or dark)

powder pigment

white vinegar

oil-base polyurethane (Last 'N Last, Minwax, or Basic Quick 15)

TOOLS

3 or more inexpensive 2" to 3"-wide natural-bristle brushes (one for the
primer, one for the polyurethane, and one for the application of each glaze
color to be used)

1 2" to 3"-wide nylon-bristle brush (for acrylic paint)

1 Badger—this and other background brushes are used to create patterns

1 multiheaded brush (a.k.a. pencil grainer)

1 metal graining comb

1 piece of stiff corrugated cardboard

1 overgrainer

1 *natural* sponge

1 small can of painter's putty (DAP or other linseed-oil putty)

1 small roll of Saran Wrap (or other plastic food wrap)

1 pair of thin latex gloves (**important**)

PRIMING

Before painting, prime the piece of furniture with BIN or any other alcohol-base or
acrylic primer. Do *not* sand the piece if an antique look is desired. Unsanded wood
will show imperfections in the final product. Sandpapering produces a smooth, slick
effect.

UNDERPAINTING

Paint the object with an acrylic semigloss paint in a color of your choice. Choose a
bright color, for the glaze you are going to apply over it will darken the base coat.
Let it dry well. Acrylic paint usually dries in about twenty to thirty minutes. For a
fine finish, coat the object twice with the semigloss paint, sanding lightly between
each application. Applying a semigloss finish is important. The glaze will then slide
on the smooth surface, making it easy to work.

GLAZE PREPARATION AND APPLICATION

Prepare the glaze mixture out of the three basic components: corn syrup (light or dark Karo syrup is recommended), white vinegar, and powder pigments. The glaze should be of a color that contrasts with the base coat. A clear glass or plastic jar enables easy observation of the mixing process, but any small container will do. Begin with 1/4 teaspoon of Karo syrup, to which you will add 1 teaspoon or more of the powder pigment. A small brush works best as it mixes the ingredients to a thick paste quickly. When thoroughly mixed, add approximately 2 tablespoons of white vinegar. Colors may be lightened or darkened by adding white, gray, or black pigment. To revive a dry glaze, add vinegar. The glaze can be thickened by adding more pigment or liquified by adding more vinegar. When using light-color pigments, you may need a larger quantity of pigment, and when using dark-color pigments, a smaller quantity.

Begin the fantasy graining technique by applying the vinegar glaze to a small area with a 2" to 3"-wide natural-bristle brush or a Badger, brushing on the glaze until it is very smooth and semitransparent. The glaze takes about five minutes to dry under normal circumstances, so you will have time to decide on the desired design motif (see the following pages for fantasy-finish alternatives). It is important to apply the glaze to an area small enough to be worked comfortably within the fast drying time of the glaze. For example, on a chest of drawers, do the top, then one side, then the other side, and then each drawer in succession. Working in this manner, the glaze will not dry out too quickly, and you won't be doing more brushing than necessary. If the glaze should dry too soon, go over the glaze with a brush that is slightly wet with vinegar, and it will be ready to work again.

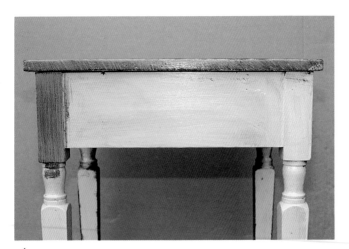

1 *A table has been primed with a base coat of yellow acrylic paint. Let it dry thoroughly.*

2 *Spread a vinegar glaze over a section of the surface with a Badger. The area glazed should be kept small so it will not dry out before the design has been completed.*

3 *Create loops with a dry #2 or #3 brush. Drag the brush to remove some of the glaze, thus allowing the yellow background to show through the loops.*

4 *Create loops with a dry #2 or #3 brush. Drag the brush to remove some of the glaze, thus allowing the yellow background to show through the loops.*

5 *With a small piece of* natural *sponge, fill in all the areas between the loops.*

6 *This is a detail of the table after the fantasy graining has been completed.*

7 *The complete table with the fantasy graining.*

CREATING THE FANTASY FINISH

Hand and Finger Fantasy Graining

Once the vinegar glaze has been applied and evenly spread over the section that you intend to work, press lightly with the undersides of your fingers to achieve a striped effect or use the tips of your fingers if you want a dotted effect. Experimenting with different parts of your hand in either an open or closed position will yield numerous variations. Press harder to provide a deeper contrast between the glaze and the underpaint. Lighter pressure removes less glaze, thus adding subtlety to the design, particularly if the hues are closely related.

1 *Apply a vinegar glaze with a Badger over a portion of the surface to be painted.*

2 *Apply a vinegar glaze with a Badger over a portion of the surface to be painted.*

3 *While it is still wet, press one fully spread hand into the glaze.*

4 *To make a wave pattern, press one hand on the wet glazed surface at regular intervals in a snakelike fashion.*

5 *Fill in the design on the remaining portion of the glaze using the fingertips.*

6 *Continue the pattern on all sides of the piece. Begin the pattern at the top of each surface and work your way down to the bottom. It is also stylish to overlap the imprinted hand pattern.*

7 *Continue the pattern on all sides of the piece. Begin the pattern at the top of each surface and work your way down to the bottom. It is also stylish to overlap the imprinted hand pattern.*

8 *Here is the finished freehand fantasy-grained cupboard that has been executed in two colors.*

Fantasy Graining with Saran Wrap

Once the glaze has been applied and evenly spread over the section that you intend to work, take a piece of Saran Wrap of about 8" in length, and loosely pleat it into narrow folds by stretching it between both hands. While holding one end in a still position on the newly glazed surface, rotate the other end, up and down in a circular motion with the other hand. A fanlike design will appear. Saran Wrap can also be pressed at random over the glazed surface to create a wood-grain background. A plastic bag or any piece of pliable plastic can be used as a substitute for the Saran Wrap.

Allow the glaze to dry thoroughly (about twenty minutes) before applying the polyurethane finish. The glazed surface will look dull when thoroughly dry.

1 Cover the surface with a vinegar glaze. While the glaze is still wet, pull out 8" of plastic wrap such as Saran Wrap.

2 Stretch the wrap to its full length, pleating it into narrow folds similar to a closed hand fan.

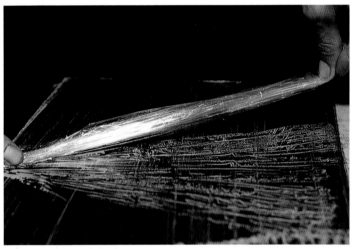

3 Gather two opposite sides of the wrap between your fingers. Resting one end of the wrap on a corner of the surface, stretch the wrap along one edge.

4 Holding the corner end of the wrap in place, rotate the far end of the wrap while lifting and dabbing the wrap at regular intervals to create a fan design.

5 Repeat the procedure at each corner of the surface.

6 Fill the center areas in a similar fashion to achieve a fully realized design.

Fantasy Graining with Putty

Once the vinegar glaze has been applied and evenly spread over the section that you intend to work, take a small quantity of putty from the can and roll it with your hands to create an elongated form. If the putty sticks to your hands, use talcum powder to remove some of the oil, or remove the excess oil by pressing the putty against a paper towel. Place the putty on the glazed surface and spread, drag, or roll it to create intricate designs. An alternative technique is to form a ball of putty and use it as a stamp, creating other fascinating patterns.

Allow the glaze to dry thoroughly (about twenty minutes) before applying the polyurethane finish. The glazed surface will look dull when thoroughly dry.

1 *Spoon out the putty from the can. Remove any excess oil by wrapping a sheet of paper towel around the putty.*

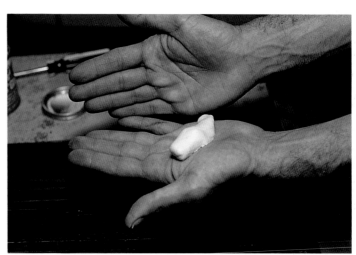

2 *Roll the putty between your hands to make it longer.*

3 *Apply the vinegar glaze to a portion of the surface that can be easily worked while it is still wet.*

4 *Press the putty over the surface with your fingertips.*

5 *A contrasting design may be achieved by holding both ends of the putty and alternately dabbing and dragging it over the wet surface.*

6 *For an interesting variation on the foregoing techniques, hold the putty at each end and roll it over the glaze.*

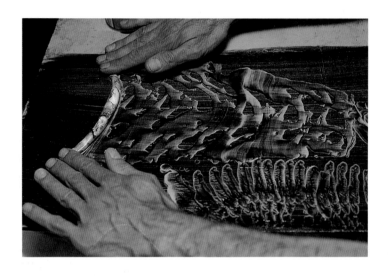

7 *For an interesting variation on the foregoing techniques, hold the putty at each end and roll it over the glaze.*

POLYURETHANE FINISH

Do **NOT** apply the polyurethane finish if you desire to erase your work, should you be dissatisfied with it. To remove the unsatisfactory glaze pattern, use a paper towel or rag saturated with vinegar. The semigloss base coat will eventually reappear. If, however, you are satisfied with the finished design, then apply the polyurethane. Apply with an inexpensive natural-bristle brush. Two or three light coats are sufficient. Allow the first coat to dry thoroughly, about two hours on a dry day, before applying the second coat. Follow the instructions on the can.

Because you have been using a water-soluble glaze, contact with anything wet will remove the glazed design, until the polyurethane finish has been applied. Polyurethane provides good water-repellant protection and will render a glossy or satin finish, depending on the type used. If you prefer to give your piece an antique look, consult chapter VII for the process to be followed.

This drop-leaf table has a background of old red acrylic paint, and the floral decoration is done freehand in black and yellow acrylic.

The top of the drop-leaf table showing the swirling flowering-vine decoration.

35

Jauntily painted with freehand red and gold acrylic decoration on a yellow background, this table has shelves that are marbleized in ocher and gray vinegar glazes on a white base. (Collection of Milton Bond)

The Saran-Wrap technique was used with a Venetian red vinegar glaze on a bright yellow background to liven this hanging box.

These two round boxes are freehand painted with acrylics. The box with the compass is in the collection of Alexander Barrett; the box with the little scene on top is in the collection of Anabelle Barrett.

On this pine trunk the canvas covering has been painted to simulate old tooled leather. Created by David Guilmet for Bell/Guilmet Design. (Photograph courtesy Olde Hope Antiques, New Hope, Pennsylvania)

The Saran-Wrap technique was used to decorate this nightstand in Venetian red over a bright yellow base. Added detailing was done with green and red acrylics.

The top of this game table has been enriched with freehand decoration done in emerald, sequin black, gold, and pearl metallic acrylic paints. The legs have been mahoganized with a black vinegar glaze over a light maroon base. (Collection of Tom Kennedy)

37

Table with raw sienna vinegar fantasy graining over a yellow background and with green and red acrylic freehand decoration.

Small table with a storage compartment having a Venetian red over yellow fantasy finish created with the Saran-Wrap and finger-painting techniques.

Bathroom vanity painted with faux-tortoise panels and drawer fronts by David Guilmet for Bell/Guilmet Design. (Photograph courtesy Olde Hope Antiques, New Hope, Pennsylvania)

Contemporary dower chest with a sponged ground and scribed design by David Guilmet for Bell/Guilmet Design. (Photograph courtesy Olde Hope Antiques, New Hope, Pennsylvania)

Document box with a fantasy finish created by William McMillen, Historic Richmond Town, Staten Island, New York.

CHAPTER V: OTHER DECORATIVE TECHNIQUES

INGREDIENTS

BIN, or other alcohol-base or acrylic primer

Acrylic semigloss paint (colors of your choice)

oil-base polyurethane (Last 'N Last, Minwax, or Basic Quick 15)

TOOLS

2 inexpensive 2" to 3"-wide natural-bristle brushes (one for the primer and one for the polyurethane)

1 2" to 3"-wide nylon-bristle brush (for acrylic paint)

3 artist brushes: #0, #3, and #5

1 roll of masking tape

1 *natural* sponge

1 candle

1 stick of chalk

1 pencil

1 straight edge or ruler

PRIMING

Before painting, prime the piece of furniture with BIN or any other alcohol-base or acrylic primer. Do *not* sand the piece if an antique look is desired. Unsanded wood will show imperfections in the final product. Sandpapering produces a smooth, slick effect.

UNDERPAINTING

Paint the object with acrylic semigloss paint in a color of your choice. Choose a color that will contrast or coordinate with the color with which you will later decorate the piece. Let it dry well. Acrylic paint usually dries in about twenty to thirty minutes. For a fine finish, coat the object twice with semigloss paint, sanding lightly between each application. For a more primitive effect, coat only once. Applying a semigloss finish will prove to be durable over time.

SPONGING

Sponging is a very old and popular technique. A *natural* sponge gives the best results because its soft and resilient texture is capable of creating exceptionally intricate designs. Cut a sponge into various sizes with a pair of scissors. Select an appropriate piece of sponge and dab it into paint that contrasts with the background. Dab the paint onto the surface of the piece and repeat the pattern at appropriate intervals.

1 *The surface here is painted with an ocher base color in acrylic.*

2 *Dab a piece of* natural *sponge into a vinegar glaze of a contrasting color such as red. It is important to use a* natural *sponge because of its soft and resilient quality.*

3 *Then dab the sponge on newspaper to remove excess paint.*

4 *Apply the sponge to the painted surface. Use heavy pressure to create bold patterns and a lighter pressure for softer designs.*

5 *To paint an arc design, dab along one edge of the surface. Starting from each sponge mark along the edge, dab on paint in an arc pattern. Patterns can be as formal or freeform as desired.*

6 *To paint an arc design, dab along one edge of the surface. Starting from each sponge mark along the edge, dab on paint in an arc pattern. Patterns can be as formal or freeform as desired.*

7 *Fill the entire area of the surface. Several colors may be used for added visual interest.*

8 *Fill the entire area of the surface. Several colors may be used for added visual interest.*

You may wish to cut your pieces of sponge into simple shapes such as hearts, houses, stars, and so forth. For a crisp imprint when sponging, always dab off excess paint onto newspaper before applying the sponge to furniture. Oversoaked sponges will leave a blurred print. Interesting results can also be obtained by alternating patterns done with sponges of various sizes. The sponging technique may also be used in conjunction with other finishes illustrated in this book to achieve wonderful folky and primitive-looking pieces.

SMOKE GRAINING

Historically popular, smoke graining is a very simple technique, but it must be done while the piece is hanging upside down. For this reason smoke graining is best achieved on small pieces. Hang the piece upside down and paint it with acrylic semi-gloss or flat paint. While the paint is still wet, pass a lighted candle underneath the piece and move it forward and backward and up and down keeping the flame away from the piece, letting only the smoke touch the surface and creating your designs with various hand movements. As the acrylic dries, the smoke will fuse and seal with it (figs. 1–4). The piece should then be polyurethaned to secure and protect the design. However, if you are dissatisfied with the smoke graining, apply another layer of acrylic paint *before polyurethaning* and begin again. Because smoke residue is black, smoke graining works best with such contrasting background colors as off-white, yellow, light blue, light green, etc.

1–3 *While the base coat is still wet, take a lighted candle and move it backward and forward and up and down under the object, keeping the flame away from the piece and letting the smoke create the decorative patterns.*

4 *Here is a small sample of decorative smoke graining.*

This drop-leaf table has a yellow undercoat, and the decorative patterning was done with smoke graining. Acrylic paint was used for the green highlights.

DECORATIVE DETAILING   Lines

Let us suppose that you have painted and grained a chest, but the look is unsatisfactory. It seems to need a bit more color or some sort of decorative detail, especially if the piece has a weak form. Adding lines to form a frame or border on the piece is a good way to make the piece more interesting. Create the lines by using masking tape. Rolls of tape can be found in many widths at local art-supply stores. Make parallel lines of masking tape that follow the shape of the piece. As a variation, create design patterns such as squares and octagons. Once tape has been applied and the design is secure, use a small section of natural sponge and dab acrylic paint in a contrasting color over the channel formed by the parallel lines of masking tape. Continue to wet the sponge as necessary. Let the paint dry and remove the tape. The decorative lines can be added over one layer of polyurethane finish. As an alternative, lines can be drawn freehand with artist brushes (#0, #3, or #5) over pencil or chalk lines. Varnish again with polyurethane, to protect the additional coats of acrylic paint.

1 *Once the painted and polyurethaned table top is completely dry, apply masking tape over the painted surface following the contour of an edge of the top.*

2 *Apply a second strip of masking tape inside and parallel to the first, thus leaving a space between the two strips for the line to be painted.*

3 *Continue applying the strips of masking tape around all the edges of the table top.*

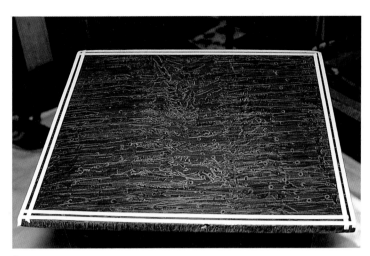

4 *The top is now completely taped.*

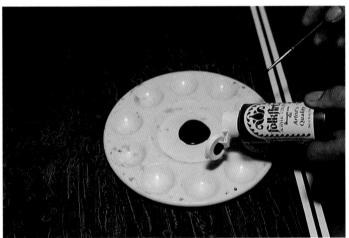

5 *Dab some acrylic paint of a contrasting color onto whatever you are using as a palette. Select a brush that has the same width of the space between the parallel strips of masking tape.*

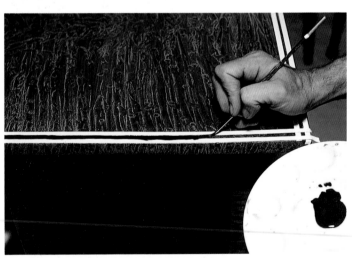

6 *Paint the area between the strips of tape and allow it to dry thoroughly.*

7 *When the paint is dry, carefully remove the strips of tape to reveal the painted line.*

8 *When the paint is dry, carefully remove the strips of tape to reveal the painted line.*

9 *Touch up any imperfect edges freehand.*

10 *Touch up any imperfect edges freehand.*

11 *Create rounded corners for additional decorative interest.*

12 *The finished table top with decorative lines.*

Highlighting

This technique is used to bring attention to the nicest parts of a piece of furniture or decorative object. For instance, if you are decorating a piece that has columns, the columns can be painted with acrylic in a color that contrasts with the rest of the piece. This will not only highlight the form of the columns but it will also create interest. Usually, some other part of the object such as drawer knobs, a drawer, or the top may also be highlighted to create a satisfying balance.

CHAPTER VI: SCENE PAINTING

INGREDIENTS

BIN, or other alcohol-base or acrylic primer

Acrylic flat or semigloss paints (in various colors of your choice). "Folk Art" paints are available in various colors in small containers at some paint or hardware stores.

oil-base polyurethane (Last 'N Last, Minwax, or Basic Quick 15)

TOOLS

2 inexpensive 2" to 3"-wide natural-bristle brushes (one for the primer and one for the polyurethane)

1 2" to 3"-wide nylon-bristle brush (for acrylic paint)

5 artist brushes (#0/2, #0, #3, #5, and #7)

1 *natural* sponge

1 pencil

When scene painting, you have the option of whether or not you wish to prime your piece. Priming yields a finished look, while an unprimed piece allows one to see the wood underneath, thus giving the finished product an older appearance (fig. 1). Using a 2" brush, apply sky-blue acrylic paint over the top one-third of the canvas or wooden surface to represent the sky (fig. 2). While the blue is still wet, place some white over various areas of the blue and blend lightly to give the appearance of clouds or a cloudy day (figs. 3, 4). Use the same brush to create water on the middle third of the canvas with a blue that is darker or lighter than the sky (fig. 5).

On the bottom third of the painting create the foreground by dipping the brush into two tones of green and some brown (fig. 6). Avoid overblending. It is better to have some light and dark areas for a more realistic look. If you use the same brush, it helps to create a more colorful and interesting effect rather than using a fresh brush each time (fig. 7).

Once the basic landscape has been completed, add the details. With a #0 artist brush, add various tree trunks (fig. 8), and with a #0/2 artist brush dipped into black paint, create the tree limbs (fig. 9). Using a small piece of *natural* sponge that you have lightly dipped into two shades of green paint (fig. 9), dab the sponge over the tree limbs to create a leafy effect. Light pressure makes a feathery, airy-looking tree (fig. 10). Heavy pressure gives a bushier effect to the tree (figs. 11, 12). Small houses can be effectively added by using various colors that contrast with the background such as white, light blue, and yellow (fig. 13).

1 *An unpainted wooden panel.*

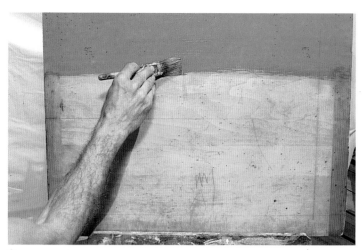

2 *With a 2" brush paint a blue base for the sky at the top of the panel.*

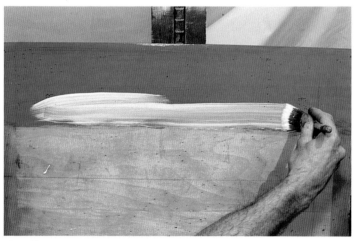

3 *Dip the same brush into some white paint and apply this whitened blue paint to the still-wet blue sky.*

4 *Blend the colors to create a cloudy effect.*

5 *With a clean brush, paint another section of the panel with a darker blue to create a body of water.*

6 *Insert land masses in the foreground by applying a blend of green and brown tones.*

7 *Insert land masses in the foreground by applying a blend of green and brown tones.*

8 *Add trees by using a #0 artist brush dipped in black or brown paint to make the tree trunks.*

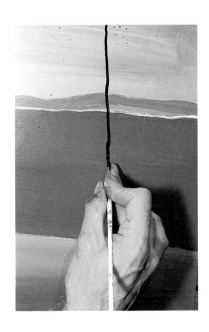

9 *Use a #0/2 artist brush to add tree limbs at appropriate natural intervals.*

10 *To create foliage, dip a natural sponge into two shades of green paint.*

11a *Dab the two shades of green paint over and around the tree limbs. Light pressure makes a feathery, airy-looking tree.*

11b *Heavy pressure gives a bushier effect to the tree.*

12 *Note the differences between the three trees.*

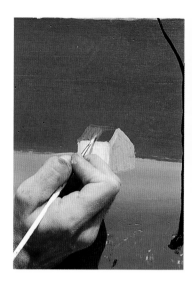

13 *Insert architectural structures, using contrasting colors such as white and red.*

To create perspective, insert small houses in the background and larger ones in the foreground. The same should be done with trees. Fences are also a good technique for creating perspective. Start the posts large in the foreground, decreasing their size as you recede further into the picture (figs. 14, 15). To give the effect of distant mountains, paint them with a very light green, or blue. This will define the distance in relation to the dark foreground of the picture (fig. 16).

A wealth of details can be added if you wish: animals (fig. 17), boats in the water (fig. 18), and birds in the sky. You should do them as you progress from one piece to the next. The first scenes you paint should be simple and easy. Details can be added after you feel comfortable with painting the basic scenery.

Folk painters are unschooled in artistic expression, so you can express yourself any way you like. The more you paint, the more confident you become. Scenes will improve in detail and realism if you just continue to paint. Even if they don't, your developing style is what is significant.

Also, it is very important to have a focal point in each picture. There should be an object or activity that attracts the viewer immediately: a large tree, an elaborate house, a lake, a river, social activity (fig. 19). Once the focal point has been established, create an interesting eye flow using other techniques of perspective, such as a receding fence or progressively smaller trees. The focal point does not have to be the most beautiful part of your scene. It simply serves to attract the viewer into your painting.

POLYURETHANE FINISH

In the case of scene painting, finishing with a coat of polyurethane is an option, since the paint cannot be removed easily. If you choose to apply polyurethane, give only one *very light* coat, and let it dry for at least thirty minutes or until dry to the touch.

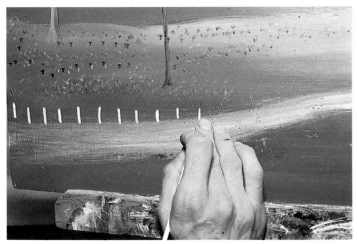

14 *Adding fenceposts of decreasing height is one technique for creating spatial depth in the painting.*

15 *Adding fenceposts of decreasing height is one technique for creating spatial depth in the painting.*

16 *Add green hills of contrasting shades to the horizon.*

17 *Animals and people may be added for interest.*

18 *Boats suggest movement and imply activity and life in a seascape.*

Here is the finished painting.

Document box enlivened with scenes in shades of blue, green, white, and black acrylic paints.

Chest of drawers that is primed and then painted in blue-green and with decorative highlights on the columns. The scenes on the drawers are in shades of green, blue, red, white, yellow, and brown. All the paints are acrylic. (Collection of Toni and Aymon DeMauro)

Chest of drawers with a base coat of salmon acrylic that is grained with an ocher vinegar glaze. The scenes are painted in tones of green and yellow acrylic with both sponges and brushes.

Detail showing scene on a drawer of the chest.

Armoire with grained paneled doors and scenic panels featuring sheep in country landscapes. The artist is Anne G. Harris. (Private collection)

Antique box with a contemporary base coat of blue, to which have been added scenes in green, blue, red, yellow, white, and brown acrylic. The box was then distressed and antiqued. (Private collection)

Single bed painted in dark green with yellow lines and with country scenes. All paints are acrylic.

Chest of drawers with freehand vines on the top and sides. The drawer fronts contain a Peaceable Kingdom scene in acrylic paint. (Collection of Grace and Bill Ryan)

Unprimed wooden box decorated with scenes in acrylic paint, and then distressed. (Private collection)

Freehand-painted folding screen of hills and trees in shades of green, yellow, red, and black acrylic.

Desk that has fantasy vinegar graining. The panel containing the freehand acrylic seascape folds down to reveal the interior of the desk, which is illustrated in the frontispiece to this book. (Collection of Tom Kennedy)

Squash court that is being primed with acrylic outdoor primer before being decorated with scenes.

Squash court. The cement was painted with outdoor acrylic paints in shades of green, sienna, red, white, blue, and brown.

CHAPTER VII: ANTIQUING

INGREDIENTS

1 large can of black shoe polish

1 large can of brown shoe polish

1 large can of neutral shoe polish

TOOLS

1 sandblock

1 package of #1 steel wool

1 roll of paper towels

several clean cotton rags

1 polishing brush (optional)

The process of antiquing requires distressing (scratching and removing) paint to expose some of the underlying wood or other layers of paint (if more than one color is desired). To begin the antiquing process, apply a thin layer of acrylic paint and then allow it to dry thoroughly (figs. 1–3). Sand lightly with a sandblock and/or #1 steel wool to remove some of the paint (figs. 4-7). The places to be distressed in this manner vary, of course, on the piece of furniture.

When antiquing a table, the places of simulated wear should reflect the areas most often touched, such as the top and surrounding edges. The tops of chests of drawers where decorative objects might have been placed, and the feet that might have decayed, darkened, or sustained paint loss over the years from floor cleanings, are also appropriate places to distress. Distress the sides of a table sparingly. Protected areas rarely show much wear.

When antiquing chairs or stools, remove substantial amounts of paint from seats so that they appear to have been well used (figs. 4 and 7). The backs of chairs, such as slatbacks, ladderbacks, and crest rails should be distressed in the places where one leans against them. The stretchers on chairs should be distressed where feet would normally rest on them (fig. 5), and the feet on chairs should be distressed where mops and brooms might have scratched the paint (fig. 6).

When you have finished distressing the object, rub a soft rag, *lightly* coated with brown shoe polish, over the entire object in an uneven manner (fig. 8). Let the polish dry for a few minutes. Spread a small amount of black shoe polish over areas that might have become more thoroughly discolored or distressed, such as table tops, seats of chairs or stools, drawer knobs on chests, table legs, chair stretchers and feet. Allow the polish to dry for a few minutes before buffing with a clean rag or brush

1 *Prime or paint the object with a contrasting color if desired.*

2 *Apply a thin layer of paint and let it dry thoroughly.*

3 *Apply a thin layer of paint and let it dry thoroughly.*

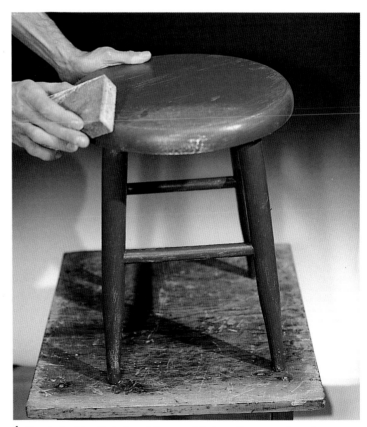

4 *Sand the object lightly with a sandblock and/or #1 steel wool to remove some of the paint, especially from areas that would normally have received wear.*

5 *Sand the object* lightly *with a sandblock and/or #1 steel wool to remove some of the paint, especially from areas that would normally have received wear.*

6 *Sand the object* lightly *with a sandblock and/or #1 steel wool to remove some of the paint, especially from areas that would normally have received wear.*

7 *Sand the object* lightly *with a sandblock and/or #1 steel wool to remove some of the paint, especially from areas that would normally have received wear.*

8 *Rub a soft rag* lightly *coated with brown and/or black shoe polish over the entire object in an uneven manner.*

9 *Allow the polish to dry for a few minutes before buffing with a clean rag or brush.*

(fig. 9). The more polish that is used, the older the object will look. The amount of distressing must naturally be left to the discretion of the artist.

It is important to be aware of the fact that shoe polish can totally change the color of your furniture. Always make a test before using it. For example, when you are working with various shades of blue, test the shoe polish on a small area before using it to cover the entire piece. Better yet, it is probably a good idea to test the shoe polish on a piece of scrap wood painted with the blue you are using. Brown shoe polish appears yellow when it is applied; therefore, if brown polish is applied over blue, the blue paint will seem to change to green. *Use only black or neutral shoe polish on blue paint.*

To achieve a soft look, use neutral shoe polish, which causes colors to change only slightly. Neutral shoe polish is also effective in lightening overly dark applications of black and brown polish. If you wish to remove the brown or black shoe polish, apply neutral shoe polish to a clean rag and rub it over the entire area to be lightened.

10 *The finished object after antiquing.*

Once it has been buffed, shoe polish will not rub off on clothing or table linen. It is as effective as furniture polish, and it remains problem free unless it is subjected to heavy cleaning products.

Left alone, painted furniture naturally develops a beautiful patina through daily use over a long period of time. However, if you are looking for fast results, shoe polish works wonders. Antiquing obviously is a subjective process, so the question of whether or not you wish to antique your furniture must remain an entirely personal choice.

Pennsylvania corner cupboard, circa 1810. Photograph courtesy Olde Hope Antiques, New Hope, Pennsylvania.

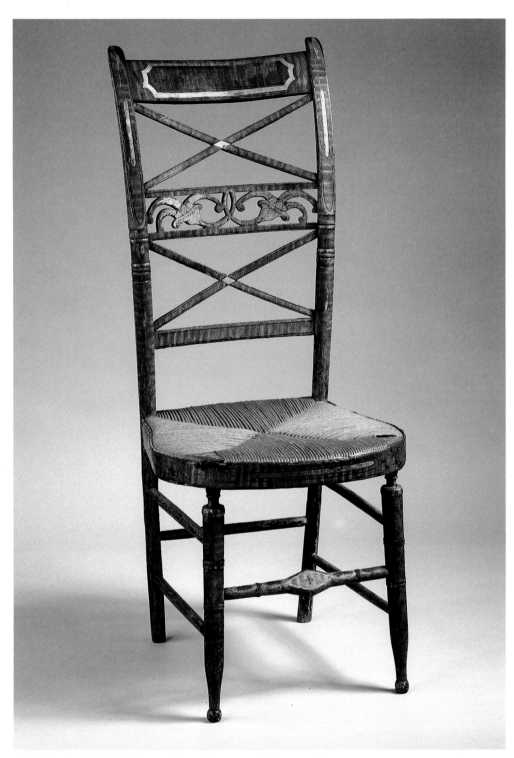

New England hall chair, early 19th century. (Collection of Burton and Helaine Fendelman)

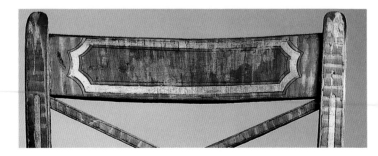

Detail of back of New England hall chair.

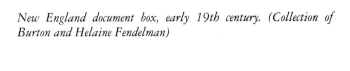

New England document box, early 19th century. (Collection of Burton and Helaine Fendelman)

New England pantry box, circa 1830. (Collection of Burton and Helaine Fendelman)

Maine Shaker sugar box, circa 1835. (Collection of Burton and Helaine Fendelman)

Pennsylvania corner cupboard with graining simulating tiger maple, circa 1830. Photograph courtesy Olde Hope Antiques, New Hope, Pennsylvania.

*Pennsylvania tilt-top candlestand, c. 1800. Photograph courtesy
Olde Hope Antiques, New Hope, Pennsylvania.*

New England side table, early 19th century. (Private collection)

New England document box, circa 1830. (Private collection)

Pennsylvania German schrank, Lancaster County, circa 1780. Photograph courtesy Olde Hope Antiques, New Hope, Pennsylvania.

Pennsylvania German schrank, Berks County, circa 1800. (Collection of Burton and Helaine Fendelman)

New York document box, early 19th century. (Collection of Burton and Helaine Fendelman)

Pennsylvania document box, early 19th century. (Private collection)

73

New England secretary, circa 1770. (Museum of American Folk Art, New York City)

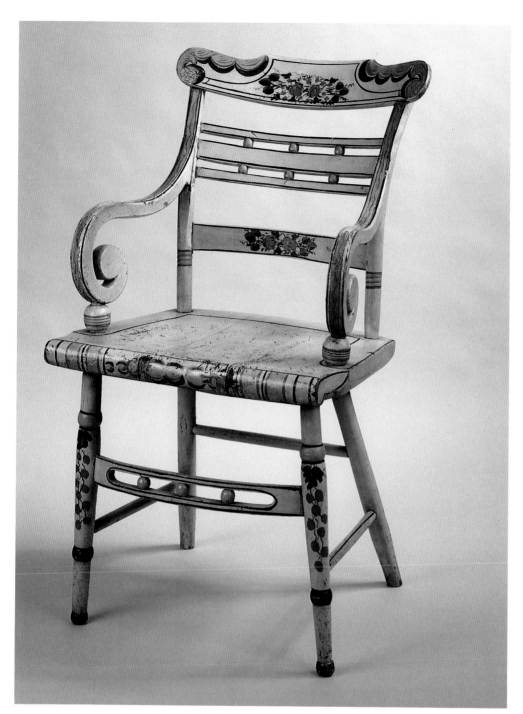

New England armchair, early 19th century. (Collection of Burton and Helaine Fendelman)

Detail of crest rail of New England armchair.

75

Connecticut tall case clock, circa 1820. (Collection of Burton and Helaine Fendelman)

New England desk, early 19th century. (Collection of Burton and Helaine Fendelman)

New England side table, circa 1830. (Museum of American Folk Art, New York City)

Detail of crest rail of Windsor side chair.

New England blanket chest with drawers, circa 1830. (Private collection)

Pennsylvania dower chest, circa 1830. (Collection of Burton and Helaine Fendelman)

Maine chest-on-chest of drawers, circa 1840. (Private collection)

Indiana Amish wardrobe, circa 1830. Photograph courtesy Olde Hope Antiques, New Hope, Pennsylvania.

New England cupboard, circa 1840. (Museum of American Folk
Art, New York City)

Vermont chest of drawers, circa 1830. (Collection of Burton and
Helaine Fendelman)

Pennsylvania German dower chest, Dauphin County, c. 1810. Photograph courtesy Olde Hope Antiques, New Hope, Pennsylvania.

New England side table, circa 1820. (Private collection)

Detail of splash board on side table.

Maryland stenciled side chair, circa 1825. (Collection of Burton and Helaine Fendelman)

Detail of crest rail of Maryland side chair.

Pennsylvania or Ohio bedstead, mid-19th century. (Collection of Burton and Helaine Fendelman)

New England room with murals by Rufus Porter, circa 1830.

New England Hitchcock armchair, circa 1825. (Private collection)

New England Windsor side chair, circa 1825. (Private collection)

Detail of crest rail of Windsor side chair.

Detail of crest rail of New England armchair.